Table of

INTRODUCTION
Chapter 1: Establishing A Routine
Chapter 2: Attention to Detail
Chapter 3: Command and Praise
Chapter 4: Teach Your Boxer To Tell You He Needs To Go Out
Chapter 5: Crate Training
Chapter 6: Housetraining a puppy when you work
Chapter 7: Housetraining overnight
Conclusion:
Resources:

INTRODUCTION
How To House Train A Boxer Puppy

Congratulations on your new Boxer puppy! If you're reading this book, this is likely your first-ever puppy or it's been a long time since you've had a puppy in the house and you need a bit of a refresher.

Not to worry. House training a Boxer is really quite easy. It does require paying attention to detail, being patient, praising your puppy and developing a predictable routine. But with these four components, your Boxer puppy will be house trained in no time.

The key thing is patience. It's similar to potty-training a baby. But unlike babies, boxers do not wear diapers (seriously, please don't consider that as an option). Just like babies need some time to learn, so do puppies. Remember, they love your attention and need it to feel that they have a value in your life. Being harsh to them every time will only lead your puppies to be either scared of you or hate you. Just like when you scold a baby every time, they get a bad memory and image of you that sticks onto their brains.

There are several methods of house training a dog and selecting the right method for your lifestyle is really important. No matter which one you choose, you still need to pay attention to details, be patient, praise your puppy and develop a predictable routine. Some training styles you may have heard of are clicker training, crate training, tether/umbilical cord training, freestyle training and punishment.

Research has demonstrated that punishment **does not work**. Urinating and defecating are natural bodily functions and it's your job to teach your puppy WHERE to do his business. If he piddles on the floor and you rub his nose in it he won't understand that his mistake was WHERE he piddled. Even worse, he may become fearful of you, and that is an unhealthy relationship between you and your puppy. The methods we'll teach you here are much more effective and will not only teach your new pooch where to poo, but will also help build that bond of trust and loyalty with you. After all, isn't that why you got your Boxer puppy in the first place?

Also remember that until you brought your puppy to your home she's likely been living with her mom and siblings – and they had different rules about where to go to the bathroom than you do. So it isn't just your pup that needs house training; it's you too. You and your pup need to learn what is expected and how to communicate that between the two of you.

Dogs are naturally clean creatures so they do not want to urinate and defecate where they sleep. That's one of the reasons many people like to crate-train their puppies. This assumes that the puppy will "hold it" longer if she's in her crate. It also assumes your puppy will sleep in the crate. Advocates of crate training equate the crate to a dog's den, where the dog feels safe inside of it. In my personal experience some of my dogs have loved their crate while others didn't embrace the whole "dog den" concept of the crate. If you opt to crate train your puppy, then you really need to adhere to the regimen needed in crate training. More on that in Chapter 5.

The next type of training is clicker training. It is just as its name suggests. You have a clicker in your hand and whenever your Boxer puppy does something right you click the clicker and give her a treat. With regards to potty training this simply means that when she goes to the bathroom in the right place, you click the clicker when she starts peeing so she equates the clicker sound with a command. But potty training to a clicker is only one aspect of clicker training. If you want to use clicker training, you should incorporate the clicker into all the training you do with your new Boxer.

Tether and umbilical cord training are two names for the same method. With this method, you 'tether' your puppy to you with a leash that's about six feet long. This method is intended to give you and your puppy some freedom of movement but doesn't allow your Boxer to wander off and tinkle somewhere while your head is turned! Some puppies will follow you anywhere and not even know they are tethered to you. Others will tug to try to get away. If you have a tugger, simply let her throw her little temper tantrum while you stand still and she will quickly learn that there's no point in tugging. If you tug back, however, she'll see this as a challenge.

Freestyle training is also exactly as its name suggests. Freestyle training combines components of all other training styles (except punishment!) and uses those that are most successful for YOUR puppy. In my experience, each dog will respond to different styles – just like my dogs who have loved the crate versus those who have hated the crate. So throughout this book we'll refer to a variety of methods you can experiment with – so select the one that your Boxer puppy responds to the best.

Chapter 1:
Establishing A Routine

Think about your own routine during a day. You get up. You go to the bathroom. You eat a meal. You go to the bathroom. You drink liquids. You go to the bathroom. Your internal "urge" tells you when to go but it is these activities that lead to that urge.

A Boxer puppy also has that urge but hasn't yet learned

    a) What that urge means

    b) How to communicate with you when that urge occurs

So to start house training your Boxer puppy you need to establish a disciplined routine that includes potty breaks.

Just like people, puppies need to go to the bathroom when they first wake up in the morning. So start your Boxer's day at his potty spot. This should be at the same time every day. Your puppy doesn't know Saturday from Wednesday so if you take your puppy out before you go to work at 6:30am during the work week, you'll need to take your puppy out at 6:30am on your weekend days too. Don't worry. Once your Boxer is a little older and house trained, she'll want to sleep in. This is just during and a little while after the house training period.

If you are training your puppy to go outside to do his business then always take him through the same door and always take him to the same part of the lawn. The more routine everything is, the faster your Boxer will become house trained.

If you're going to create a spot inside your home for your puppy to use as his bathroom, then place it where you plan to have it for his entire life. You don't want to start off with his Dog Potty in the kitchen because it's close to his food only to move it to the laundry room when he's older.

Once you bring your puppy inside you'll want to feed her and give her water. I strongly encourage you to stay with her while she eats and drinks. That way you'll know when she's finished and you'll know when she needs to urinate. Typically, a puppy needs to go to the bathroom about 10-15 minutes after she's eaten. Once she's finished eating, note what time it is and pick up her food AND water bowl. Take her to her potty spot 10 minutes later.

You need to distinguish between play time and pee time. So while you're at her potty spot, the expectation is she will go to the bathroom. Don't talk to her until she starts to urinate. AFTER she has begun to urinate/defecate, give her a verbal command, like "Potty" or "Wet" or "Tinkle." If you command before she begins she won't associate your command with the function of peeing so this timing is *really important*. It's also critical that you use the same command each time. Even if you think of "tinkle" as urinating, it can also mean defecating for the purposes of house training your Boxer puppy.

When she is finished, praise her as if she has just accomplished a feat unlike any other. Let her hear your praise in the tone of your voice. You may consider giving her a small treat that you've brought in your pocket for just this moment. Or reward her with a few minutes of playtime. If you have a fenced in yard, throw the ball or a stick for her to chase.

Again, remember that routine is critical so figure out what your Boxer puppy considers to be the best reward (food, your love or some playtime) and use that same type of reward every time he goes to the bathroom.

Until your puppy is about 3 months old, she'll need to go out every 2 – 5 hours. Obviously that's a big gap, so now comes the "trial and error" period of house training. If you're at home all day with your Boxer, then take her out every two hours. Keep in mind to take her out the same door to the same area in the yard and don't talk with her until she begins to urinate and then give your verbal (or clicker) command.

If he doesn't potty right away give him 5 minutes or so but you stay quiet. If he still doesn't go, take him inside. Make a mental note that your puppy can go longer than two hours. Wait about 10 minutes (watching him all the time) and take him out again. Do exactly the same thing; walk him to the Potty Spot, don't say anything until he starts to pee. While he's peeing, state your command out loud (or click the clicker) and reward him enthusiastically for his success.

If your Boxer puppy wets when you bring him in the house, don't fuss at him. Instead, say something like, "Woops!" in a surprised voice. That should catch his attention enough to stop his wetting. Then pick him up and take him out to his Potty Spot to finish his business. If he doesn't stop when you say "Woops!", then don't react to him wetting in the house. When he's finished, just clean it up and make a mental note that his time between pees is about 2:10.

Make note of the time, plan to give him a bowl of water in 2 hours and plan to take him out again in 2 hours and 10 minutes.

Test your Boxer puppy's timing to see if she needs to go out every 2 hours, every 2 ½ hours, every 3 hours, etc. Whatever it is, be sure that's how frequently you take her out. Don't delay. Remember, routine, routine, routine. That's what's going to get your puppy housetrained the most quickly. If you miss the time to take your puppy out, don't get angry with your pup. If you must get angry, get angry at yourself.

Most puppies eat three times a day so you'll want to take her out 10 minutes after she eats lunch, once between lunch and dinner and then again after dinner. Plan to take her out right before bedtime and until she's 3 months old you should plan to take her out once throughout the night too.

To recap, expect your Boxer puppy to need to go out every 2-5 hours during the day and every 4-5 hours through the night until she's 3 months old. By 3 months old she should be sleeping through the night so you take her out right before bedtime and again upon getting up.

Your Boxer puppy's bedtime should be as regimented as her getting up time. Same time every night, no matter whether it's a weekday or a weekend.

Here's an example schedule:

6:00am	wake up and go out
6:45am	breakfast food and drink (15 minutes to eat) pick up food and water
7:10am	go out
9:00am	set out water bowl for puppy to have a drink
9:10am	go out
11:10am	go out
12:00noon	food and drink (15 minutes to eat) pick up food and water bowl
12:25pm	go out
2:15pm	set out water bowl for puppy to have a drink
2:25pm	go out
4:25pm	go out
5:30pm	food and drink (15 minutes to eat) pick up food and water bowl
5:55pm	go out
7:30pm	set out water bowl for puppy to have a drink
7:40pm	go out
7:45pm	go to bed
12:30am	go out and then straight back to bed

Of course if you play vigorously with your puppy, be sure to give him a drink of water afterward – and also be sure to take him to his Pee Spot 10 minutes after drinking the water!

While your ultimate goal may be to simply open the door and have your dog go out on his own, this won't be the case in the beginning. You *must* escort your puppy to her Potty Spot. And while this schedule may appear to be too regimented, those who maintain a strict schedule will achieve house training most quickly.

Chapter 2:
Attention to Detail

During the potty training stage it's really important that your Boxer puppy is ALWAYS where you can see him. That way you can watch his behavior and within no time at all you'll recognize his particular clues that will tell you he's about to pee or poo.

It'll take a few days for you to really understand his clues. For example, if he starts sniffing around that might be a sign that he needs to go out. But it could also simply be a puppy being curious. Don't be too quick to scoop her up and run outside. But if, over the course of two or three days, you notice the *only time* she sniffs the floor is when she's about to pee, then you know she's providing you with a clue that she needs to go outside.

Another clue is if you are playing together and she stops playing all of a sudden and starts walking away from you. Puppies generally don't stop playing until they're tired. And if that's the case, they'll usually just curl up right at your feet; not go off somewhere.

And the obvious clue is if he starts to squat. Remember NOT to yell, but use your "surprise!" voice just to catch his attention. In this instance, absolutely scoop him up and take him out to his Pee Spot. During the housebreaking phase it's important to have a pet odor neutralizer to clean with. Honestly, puppy pee doesn't really have a bad odor to humans, but you want to clean it up so your Boxer puppy can't smell it. If he can smell it, he'll think that's an appropriate Pee Spot and you certainly don't want that!

Another detail you need to pay attention to is feeding time. Dogs that eat at the same time every day poop at the same time every day. In the long run you're job of potty training will be a lot easier if you make sure your Boxer is fed on a strict schedule. Since eating and pooping go hand in hand, it's important that you pick the puppy's food bowl up when she's finished eating. If she leaves any food in her bowl, you can leave it down for about 10 minutes. If she doesn't return in that 10 minutes, pick it up. That 10 minute mark is the time you're taking her out to her Pee Spot anyway so those two details go hand in hand as well.

If you leave the food bowl on the floor with food in it and she goes back at a later time to eat what she left, then she'll need to poop again. But if you don't see her eat those left overs, she might be pooping in your kitchen.

Are you starting to see a pattern here? It really isn't difficult to house train a puppy. The hardest part is disciplining yourself to pay attention to the details and stay on the schedule.

But we all know that sometimes life gets in the way and you can't just sit there and watch your new puppy. This is when you want to use a puppy gate or crate. The purpose of either of these is to keep your puppy safe while you tend to other things. So it's an absolute rule that if you're going to crate train your Boxer, then you must not ever use the crate as punishment. It is not the place for "time out."

Remember, puppies do not learn from being punished. If you need to crate her while you make a bed or run upstairs to do a chore, then when you return to the room her crate is in, immediately take her out of the crate and take her out to her Pee Spot. This detail is never to be overlooked or you'll likely be cleaning up pee. You don't need to fuss over her or even praise her for having been a good girl in her kennel. We're working toward making her crate a place she enjoys being, so what's the big deal hanging out in a place she likes to hang out for an hour or so? But since dogs rarely go to the bathroom where they sleep, if she does get the urge to pee while she's in the crate, if you don't take her to her Pee Spot right away when she comes out of the crate, she'll go pee in the house.

Set her up for success, not failure by always, always, always taking her to her Pee Spot the minute you open the crate door.

If your Boxer puppy doesn't like the crate, then consider getting a puppy gate or puppy pen. You can use the puppy gate to block off a room so the puppy feels like she has room to roam but you won't have to go looking for her under couches or behind dressers (both easy places to pee really fast, by the way). If you opt for the puppy gate, the best room to confine your puppy to is one with a laminate or tile floor, if you have one. It's much easier to clean up puppy pee/poo than on carpet.

The other product is the one my current dog was trained with when she was a puppy. It's the puppy pen. Unlike a child's play pen it doesn't have a bottom in it and the sides aren't made of mesh. Rather it's more like a gate that is pliable and you can make it in the form of a circle and you can make it bigger or smaller, depending on the space you have available. My current dog loved this when she was a puppy because she could be in whatever room I was in. But my other dog, when he was a puppy, hated it because he could see me but couldn't get to me. He was much happier in his crate.

Whether it's a crate, a puppy gate or a puppy pen, commit to finding the one your Boxer is most comfortable with and you'll have no problems putting her there when you can't pay attention to her every detail.

Chapter 3:
Command and Praise

Dogs are pack animals and a new puppy needs a leader who will make him feel safe and secure. *You* are that pack leader for him and you need to communicate your own confidence so the Boxer puppy knows his leader "has his back."

COMMAND AND PRAISE: The way you demonstrate your leadership is through the way you command and praise your puppy. One without the other is ineffective. It confuses your puppy and you don't get the results you want. Barking orders without rewarding with praise or praising your pup without first providing a command is confusing to the puppy. He thinks, "My leader yelled at me, I did what I thought she wanted me to do" but without the feedback of praise the puppy is left uncertain. Similarly, if you do not give the command "pee" when the puppy starts to wet but you do say "Good Girl Sadie" when she's finished, she isn't sure why she's receiving the praise. Is it for peeing? Is it for being still? Is it for stopping peeing? You can see, I'm sure, how the puppy is left confused.

When you command and praise your new Boxer you are teaching him that what he has done is indeed what you wanted him to do. It also reinforces that you are the leader/teacher and he is the follower/student and in order for him to receive praise, he must do what you tell him to do.

If you don't train your puppy to obey you then she will train you to obey her. That's right. If you think your puppy will obey you because you feed her, take her out to go poo and play with her then she's in control. She needs to understand that in order to get what *she* wants, she has to do what *you* want.

Many people are uncomfortable with the word "command" or feel like they are being mean to a puppy by using a stern voice and telling them what to do. I assure you, this is not the case. Your Boxer puppy will grow up to be a confident, secure dog as a result of you providing clear commands and lavishing your praise on him when he does what you tell him to do.

Think about the first job you ever had. You didn't know what to do. If you had a good boss, he told you what you were expected to do. You took a stab at doing the task. Your boss then reviewed your work and told you if you had done it right or wrong and you became a confident, productive employee.

If you had a bad first boss, they shook your hand and welcomed you to the company and left you on your own to figure out what you were supposed to do. You stumbled a lot in the beginning and had to watch your colleagues to figure out what the expected behavior was. The job was likely frustrating and disappointing.

The same holds true for your new Boxer. And if he doesn't have any "colleagues" (he's the only dog in the house) he'll be very uncertain, stressed and timid because he'll have no idea how to behave.

Tell him what you expect him to do and give him tons of praise when he does what he's supposed to do.

COMMAND AND PRAISE.

Timing is everything when it comes to praise and this is especially true when housetraining your new puppy. The first few days you are housetraining you'll pick the puppy up and carry her to her Pee Spot. But as time goes on, you'll expect her to walk to her Pee Spot, then you'll expect her to tell you when she needs to go out.

It's helpful for the puppy if you do what you expect her to do in the next two steps. In other words, when you pick her up to take her to her Pee Spot, make a verbal command. Perhaps your verbal command is "Out." So you say "out" pick up the pup and walk outside.

Let's say your ultimate expectation is your puppy will scratch at the door when she needs to go out. So you say "out" as you pick up your puppy, when you get to the door you scratch it, then walk through it.

You should carry your puppy to her Pee Spot until she's three months old. By then she should have some bladder control. Before the age of three months old, she may be walking with you to the door when the urge to pee hits her and then she pees right there inside the door! This confuses so many first time puppy owners. "She was at the door! Why did she pee INSIDE?" She peed inside because she doesn't have enough bladder control to hold it. So until she's three months old, carry her to her Pee Spot.

Once at her Pee Spot, set your puppy down and become a statue until she starts to pee. While she is peeing you command, "Pee" and immediately when she is finished you praise her lavishly.

If you need to pick up her poo, be sure you praise her FIRST and then pick up the poo. If you pick up the poo first and then praise her she won't know what she's being praised for. You have five seconds to begin praising your Boxer puppy in order for her to make the connection between peeing and being rewarded.

Vary the way you praise your Boxer so she continues to be excited by your praise. If you've been married any length of time you know what I mean. When you first started dating and maybe even when you first got married, if you were leaving the house for work and your spouse shouted behind you, "Bye. I love you!" it pleased you. But if you're married and your spouse calls out "I love you" every time you go to work, it is predictable and carries less meaning. Not because your spouse doesn't mean it. And not because you don't like hearing it. But it's now just part of the routine when you leave for work. If you've been married five years, that means your spouse has called "I love you" 1,200 mornings and most likely when you hit the exact same spot in your path to the front door. What would happen if one day he said, "Bye honey. You look gorgeous today."

So switch up the way you praise your puppy so it doesn't become routine. To help you get started, here are

Ten Ways To Praise Your Puppy While Potty Training

1. Scratch her behind the ear

2. Use your "happy voice" and say "good girl Sadie" (always use her name) Your praise voice should be a pitch or two higher than your normal voice

3. Say "Let's Play Sadie!" Play for a few minutes; throw a ball or a stick or run around together

4. Pat her on the chest (this builds a dog's confidence)

5. Give her a treat (very small –about the size of a green pea) Have them in your pocket and give verbal praise while giving her the treat

6. Rub her neck from behind the collar and down her side to the hind leg

7. Clap for her and say "Way to go Sadie"

8. Give her a big hug and say, "You rock Sadie"

9. Squat down and look her in the eye and give her a verbal praise (Some trainers say that looking a dog in the eyes is an aggressive cue in the dog pack. However, I have looked my dogs straight in the eyes since I got them and in 45 years of dog ownership I have never had a bad experience in doing so. I usually get a lick for it!)

My dog's favorite is when I give her a good scratch up and down her sides and back

How NOT To Praise Your Puppy

Many people have a tendency to pat or pet a puppy on the head. This is actually an aggressive move in doggie-language. It isn't a reward. It says to the puppy, "I am dominant over you." While you want the puppy to know you are the leader, you want to be a kind, confident, gentle leader; not a bully.

Don't stand over your Boxer. This is another sign of dominance that will more likely lead to your puppy being fearful of you instead of respectful of you.

Chapter 4:
Teach Your Boxer To Tell You He Needs To Go Out

Congratulations! Your puppy is peeing and pooping on schedule. She's even "holding it" so that she can walk to her Pee Spot instead of you having to carry her there.

Now it's time to teach her how to tell you she wants to go out. Ideally, you've been showing her this all along the way. In Chapter 3 we discussed how, when you carry your Boxer puppy out, you scratch the door as you go through it. That was you teaching her the command to go out. By three months old she may be scratching the door on occasion. If so, I hope you're giving her tons of praise for it. She's a fast learner!

Many dog owners swear by the bell. In other words, they train their puppy to ring a bell with his nose to indicate he wants to go out. I've personally tried this with five dogs and my dogs scratch the door next to the bell! But every dog is different so if your Boxer puppy doesn't get the scratching command; she might "get" the bell.

Get some "sleigh bells" at a craft shop and attach them to a ribbon or piece of cord and hang it near the door that leads to the Pee Spot. Each time you take your puppy to her Pee Spot, be sure to ring the bell. Then when she's ready to learn how to tell you she wants to go out, follow the instructions below.

    1. Place some very small treats in your pocket.

    2. Take the bells off the wall and rub one of the treats on them to get the treat scent on the bells.

    3. Place the bells very close to your Boxer's nose. Close enough that she can get a whiff of the treat smell. She'll likely move forward and hit the bells with her nose.

    4. When she hits the bell say "YES" with tons of enthusiasm and give her a treat.

    5. Do this about 10 times.

    6. Repeat twice a day for two-three days.

Let's assume you've been using the command "out" when you stepped through the door to go to the Pee Spot.

    1. Once your Boxer puppy absolutely "gets" that she's supposed to poke

the bells with her nose, move the bells a bit further away from her. When she moves forward and pokes the bell, replace the word "YES" with the word "OUT". Continue to reward her with the treats.

2. Put the bells beside her instead of in front of her. When she pokes the bell, command "OUT" and reward her.

3. Slowly work your way toward the door you go out as you do this training exercise. Repeat twice a day for three-five days.

Remember to return the bells to their spot by the door and continue to ring the bell when you take your puppy out during this training period.

1. Once he's gotten the hang of ringing the bell, it's time for him to ring the bell at the right time and for the right reason.

2. Again, with treats in your pocket, when it's time to go to the Pee Spot, put the puppy down inside, by the bells and command "OUT".

3. He touches the bell with his nose, you give him a treat and then you WALK him to his Pee Spot. No more carrying. No more free rides! He's old enough to "hold it" until he gets to his Pee Spot and he's ringing the bell on his own. You, however, are still managing when he goes out.

This phase will take two-to-three months before you can rely on your Boxer puppy to ask to go out every time he needs to pee. So continue with a schedule of trips outside; although not near as frequently as it was when you first got your puppy.

Continue to stop at the door and command "OUT" and have your puppy ring the bell or scratch the door.

Some dogs actually paw at the bell instead of using their nose. That's OK. As long as he's making those bells ring.

One note of importance – do NOT hang the bell on the door handle if you ever use that door for anything other than going to the Pee Spot. Otherwise the bells will ring every time you open or close that door, which will definitely be confusing to your puppy.

Some dog authorities say you don't need to train your Boxer to tell you when she needs to go out. If you create a regimented schedule, your puppy will learn to "hold it" until it's time to go out. If you subscribe to this, though, you must follow that schedule for the rest of the dog's life. That's why I prefer to teach a puppy to tell me when she needs to go out and pee.

Chapter 5:
Crate Training

Crate training is exactly as its name implies, you use a specially-designed-for- dogs crate to train your Boxer puppy. Being in the crate is not punishment for your puppy; it's his safe haven, his den, his crib. Make it comfortable and a place he wants to be.

If used correctly, as your puppy grows up she will want to go in her crate and you'll need to keep the crate door open so she can get in as opposed to keeping it closed so she can't get out!

But back to housetraining your puppy using a crate.

When crate training, you'll still need to create a regimented schedule, like the example schedule in Chapter 1. When you are not feeding your puppy, playing with her or taking her outside to pee and poop you'll put your puppy in her crate. She'll take her naps in the crate and have her "down time" in the crate.

In Chapter 1 example schedule, it does not outline play and cuddle time. But you do need to factor these into a schedule if you're going to crate train your puppy. Don't just take her out of her crate to eat, drink, poop and pee!

When you select a crate, it needs to be big enough for your Boxer puppy to stand up in and turn around in. Of course, the size crate you need for a six week old puppy is certainly smaller than the size of crate you'll need full a full grown Boxer.

So you have two options. The first option is to plan to buy increasingly bigger crates as your puppy grows. The second option is to buy a crate for a full size Boxer to begin with and section it off as your puppy grows. Using this method, you'll typically use only half the crate to begin with. Before you put the top on the crate, take a piece of cardboard that fits tightly into the sides of the crate and place it in the middle of the crate. Fill the back side of the crate with something like a blanket or a box with a blanket in it. Something that will prevent the puppy from pushing the "wall" down.

Now you have a crate that's half the size, which should be just the right amount of room for your Boxer puppy. If it's too much room, adjust where you place the "wall." If you give the puppy too much room she may use a corner to pee in and the other space to lay it. Make it small enough that if she pees in there she'll be too close to the pee to be comfortable laying in the crate.

Then place a dog bed or dog pad in the part he'll be laying on so that it's soft, warm and comfortable. Add a toy that the puppy can cuddle with like a baby cuddles with a teddy bear at night and your Boxer puppy should love his new den.

Where you place the crate in the house is a bit of trial and error. Some puppies are happier if the crate stays in the same place all the time, so you might want to put it in your bedroom, if that's where you plan to have your puppy sleep at night. Others prefer to have their crate wherever you are, so if you put the crate in your family room or kitchen during the day and your bedroom at night; that will work for a puppy with this temperament. Again, the key is consistency.

Whenever you take your Boxer out of the crate, immediately go to your Pee Spot. And right before you put her in her crate, be sure you take her to her Pee Spot.

Do not put her in her crate after eating or drinking, even for the 10 minutes you're waiting to take her to her Pee Spot. It's too easy for an accident to happen and you don't want her to avoid her crate because she had an accident in there. That 10 minutes between eating/drinking and going pee is a great time for you guys to play together.

I personally like to cuddle with my puppy after bringing her in from peeing and before putting her in her crate. This way she doesn't relate coming inside to being separated from you. A few minutes of cuddle time with you can be the difference between loving her crate and hating it.

Apart from the training times, try to spend as much time with your Boxer as possible as they love human company. In case you find that your Boxer pup is not responding well to your training commands, you may want to check with a good veterinarian doctor if the health of your puppy is okay or what is it that he wants which you are not able to understand.

Chapter 6:
Housetraining a puppy when you work

Bringing a new Boxer puppy into your home requires a change in your habits. Of course you want the puppy to *fit into your schedule* but there are some adjustments you will need to make. A puppy simply cannot be left alone from 8am – 5pm. She will need to eat, drink, play, pee and poo in that time period. He'll also need socialization.

While this book isn't about socialization, I must say that socialization is a critical aspect of introducing your puppy into your life and, according to the American Veterinary Society on Animal Behavior, the first three months are the most critical months in terms of dog socialization. *"Because the first three months are the period when sociability outweighs fear, this is the primary window of opportunity for puppies to adapt to new people, animals, and experiences. Incomplete or improper socialization during this important time can increase the risk of behavioral problems later in life including fear, avoidance, and/or aggression. Behavioral problems are the greatest threat to the owner-dog bond."*

This doesn't mean you can't work a fulltime job and have a puppy. But you do need a plan for caring for your Boxer puppy while you're at work.

Puppy Day Care – Just like child care, there are puppy day care centers popping up around the country. These centers thrive because so many working people have dogs. Some doggy day care centers have special programs for puppies. And, though expensive, if you can afford it, this is the way to go. You aren't only paying for the day care, you're also paying for training.

For example, there's a dog day care center in Oakland CA called Pride and Pedigree that offers a "Puppy Head Start" program. It's available as a half day program or an all-day program. They have "mentor dogs" who help teach puppies how to behave properly as a dog in a people world! They also provide basic beginning obedience training and they have a puppy gym with toys and equipment especially intended for puppies.

And as important as all of that is, they help you house train your Boxer puppy. They use the crate training method, so if you choose to enroll your puppy in a daycare that uses crate training, you should also use crate training at home at night. The consistency in training methods, which yield earlier positive results than if you used a different method than your puppy day care.

Dog Sitter – There are two levels of sitter you can hire for your puppy. One is a certified dog sitter who is trained to work with dogs and the other is a local teenager who will keep your puppy company and take her outside on the schedule you provide. If you have kids, think of it like the difference between a nanny and Saturday baby sitter. If you want to find a professional dog sitter who is also a trainer, visit Pet Sitters International to start your search.

Worse-case option - If you can't afford to take your Boxer puppy to day care or have a dog sitter come in for the first five months of your puppy's life, I'd recommend that you reconsider getting a puppy. That doesn't mean you can't have a dog. Think about adopting an older dog. That's a "whole-other" book, but adopting an older dog is a great alternative to a puppy for working households.

However, if you insist on getting a puppy and you don't use puppy day care or a dog sitter, then you and/or someone you know must go home three times during the day to feed, water, exercise and socialize your puppy and then have her do her business before you put her back in her crate, puppy playpen or gated room. Let's not beat around the bush. Anything short of this is cruelty and abuse.

Avoid leaving your Boxer puppy for long periods of time. See to it that it sees faces of family members through the day, and stays close to family and children in house. Else an abandoned and tied Boxer will get aggressive and try to bark and bite, which is quiet contrary to its normally friendly and playful nature.

Chapter 7:
Housetraining overnight

All along we've talked about taking your Boxer puppy outside to do her business every couple of hours so what happens during the night? I'm sorry to tell you, you have to set your alarm and taking your puppy out in the middle of the night. But don't worry – it won't be for long.

And the good news is, puppies can "hold it" longer when they're asleep than when they're awake. But they can't hold it all night long. If you follow the example schedule in Chapter 1, your Boxer puppy will go to her Pee Spot at 7:40pm and into her crate at 7:45pm to go to sleep.

Then you'll set your alarm for 12:30am, get up and take her to her Pee Spot, where she may still seem asleep while she pees. You still need to verbalize the command "pee" and then praise her when she's finished. But praise in the middle of the night should be calmer than it is during the day. Perhaps picking her up, nuzzling your face into her neck and whispering in a high voice, "Good Girl Sadie. Good Girl."

Carry her back to her crate, put her in it, and both of you should be back to sleep in no time.

Set the alarm again for 6:00am, wake your sleeping beauty in her kennel and carry her to her Pee Spot to start your new day.

If you are going to crate train your puppy, you may want to put her crate next to your bed at night to start with. That way if she does wake up and stir because she needs to go out, you'll hear her. Then you should take her out, no matter what time it is, because she won't be able to hold it until the scheduled time to go out. The other benefit to having the crate next to your bed is that your Boxer puppy can hear you breathing. This will bring her comfort, especially in those first few nights with you. She's used to sleeping with her mom and her siblings so the first few nights all by herself are going to be scary.

Many people like their pets to sleep with them in their beds. If you want your new Boxer puppy to sleep with you, I recommend that you put a puppy bed in your bed to start with.

Just like a crate, if your puppy has an entire bed to move around on, he might pee in one corner and sleep in the other. If you put your puppy inside a puppy bed on your bed, then he'll feel like he's sleeping with you but will not pee in his part of the bed, which is just the puppy bed. Once he's house trained he won't need to stay in the puppy bed on your bed. He may choose to, though. Or he may start climbing out of it to lay in a different spot on your bed. Then it's up to you to decide if that's acceptable or if he needs to stay in the dog bed on your bed. Being creatures of habit, if you allow him to go outside of the dog bed, you should remove the dog bed so he can sleep in the spot that the dog bed used to be on.

CPSIA information can be obtained
at www.ICGtesting.com
Printed in the USA
BVHW042257270822
645705BV00003B/357